An Article about Black and Other Walnuts

by

Carroll D. Bush

THE BLACK AND OTHER WALNUTS

The walnut species are widely distributed. If we take the record of plant studies at this time, four are native to the United States, three to Mexico, one to Cuba, two to Japan, one to north Asia, and one to Australia. One has even been reported from Africa. Prospective growers in the north who seek nuts of real value have three to consider besides the English walnut. These three are the American black walnut, the American butternut and the Japanese heartnut.

The black walnut tree furnishes us with one of the finest cabinet woods of the world. It is also valuable for gunstocks, few being made of any other wood. On account of its value for timber the native trees have been mostly cut. However it is fast growing, for a hard wood tree, and adaptable to soils and location holds its own vigorously in the wild so that it is a useful tree for forest work and will always be with us in quantity.

The black walnut is as American as maple

sugar. With its distinctive flavor it is the most superb cooking nut that could be imagined. While other nuts when cooked, become bits that cannot be identified, the flavor of a black walnut does not cook out but permeates cakes and candies with a flavor and odor distinctly its own. Of course, as with all unusual flavors, it is those who have learned its taste when children that appreciate it as they get older. The nut meats have a place in our market and are often mixed with meats from the English walnut for the bakeries and candy makers, often as much as three parts of English walnuts to one part of black walnuts. The cheaper English walnut kernels furnish the body but the black walnut kernels the flavor.

The demand for black walnut meats should grow in importance but the great foreign population of our cities knows nothing of the real America and care less. Foreigners are often the bakers and candy makers, the cooks in the fine hotels and in the cheap beaneries, and are also much of the buying public. The generation of American youth grown in the cities, too, is ignorant of American backgrounds and traditions of the bountiful American table. We find black walnut flavoring on the market, probably made from coal tar, but we do not have to use it. We should strive to hold fast those things that are good—those distinctive things of rural America that our parents and grandparents knew and proved to be good.

The American black walnut is found native from the shores of the Atlantic west to Nebraska and from Minnesota south to the Gulf States. The California black walnut is found in the valleys of California, and is separated again into two varieties—the southern California black and the northern California black. The nut of the southern black is small. The rock walnut is native to western Texas, New Mexico and Arizona. The American black is the most valuable nut though some of the nuts of the California black are good. California black walnuts are milder in flavor than the blacks from the Eastern States. For this reason, when sold in the market, as a few have been, the meats are not so much in demand by the bakeries as are the American black walnuts.

The average black walnut is hard to crack and the kernels are not too easy to get out of the shells. They come out in pieces, sometimes in halves. Due to the demand for black walnut meats many people who live in the hills of the central states, where native trees are yet to be found in quantity, make a part of their living by gathering and selling the nuts. There is considerable work in cracking and selling the meats but since the in-

FIGURE 24—BLACK WALNUTS

Three types of black walnuts that have found favor with growers in various states. *Left*, Thomas, a fast growing tree with a large nut that cracks fairly well; *center*, Stabler, a slower growing, but more compact tree with a fine cracking nut; *right*, Ohio, a moderately fast growing tree which in some sections bears well filled nuts of good quality.

vention of crackers that can handle the black walnuts much of this work is being done in cracking plants where the cracked nuts move forward on a belt and the meats are picked out by women and girls.

Where the walnut is not native as in many of the western states it was carried by the white settlers. One of my early recollections was when my father and I drove sixteen miles in a lumber wagon from our prairie home in Minnesota to the woods and brought back small trees of the black walnut. When I was older these trees furnished sacks of nuts that we stored and used during the winter. It was my job to husk and spread the nuts to dry on a shed roof. We had the imported walnuts, filberts and almonds only on holidays.

The one big improvement that we would all like in the black walnut is to make it a thin shelled, better cracking nut from which we could get the kernels, in halves if possible. For this reason a search has been made over the country for better varieties by men interested, particularly by members of the Northern Nut Growers Association. Contests have been held and thousands of nuts have been sent in and tested. A few hundred have been named and grafted and are being grown in plantings of the nut men. The nurserymen have taken a few that have been tested out fully and grafted them. Grafted trees of reliable varieties can be found in most sections of the country.

To illustrate what an improvement the better varieties are over the average seedling, Dr. N. F. Drake of Fayettesville, Arkansas, who applies a grading system to nuts, finds that the average seedling variety of black walnut runs 18 per cent kernel and the rest shell, while the better grafted varieties run 34 per cent kernel or nearly twice as much.

Although having a good cracking nut is the first test of a black walnut tree, a variety to be worth while should also have several other qualities. The Northern Nut Growers are doing further good work in checking upon the named varieties in various sections of the country, as to their hardiness, growth and bearing. These, of course, are fully as important as the nut in a commercial grove and important too if the tree is to be used for the home grove.

Of all the varieties the Thomas, one of the first introduced still leads in favor over the country. It is a large nut and while not as thin shelled as many, it cracks out fairly well. It is a fast grower, heavy bearer, and hardy, as far North as St. Paul, Minnesota. The only weakness it has ever shown is that it does not seem to do as well in low wet land as some other varieties. It seems to be self-pollinizing, though it may not be wholly so, nor in all sections.

The Stabler, which originated in Maryland is one of the best cracking nuts. It is not a fast grower and in some places it has not done well. Some growers have had good results with the Stabler and some fine nuts have been shown from trees in various parts of the country. It has been

FIGURE 25—THE ORIGINAL STABLER TREE

The Stabler black walnut, growing in Howard County, Maryland, was discovered by Henry Stabler, of Fairfax, Virginia. It is a good instance of how the country has been combed to find trees that produce better than average nuts.

favored in some windy sections as it makes a much more compact tree than some of the faster growing varieties.

The Ohio seems to stand a little shorter season than the Thomas and is preferred by a few. It is

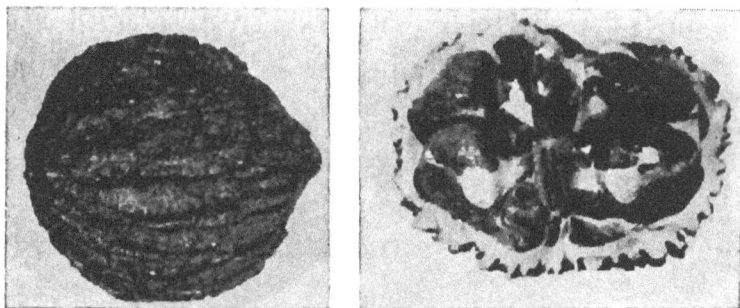

FIGURE 26—THOMAS BLACK WALNUT

Thomas black walnut showing its regular type, comparatively thin shell and a well colored full kernel.

a good cracking nut and full meated. The trees bear well.

Stambaugh and Rohwer seem to be doing well in Iowa and Minnesota where hardy trees are needed.

The Tasterite, a good cracking nut, comes from northern New York and ripens in those cooler sections where some other varieties fail to mature their nuts.

The Sifford, a recent introduction from the hills of Virginia, is a good sized nut with a large percentage of kernel, cracks well and bears well. Judging from its place of origin it may not be as hardy as some others.

From the writer's observation, the nut which has cracked best and come out of the shell most freely is the Snyder. The thinnest shell black is the Elmer Myers and the largest black walnut is the Todd. A walnut from Georgia, the Macedonia, shows a *soft* shell, quite unusual in a black walnut and has forty-three per cent kernel.

The Snyder is being propagated by some eastern nurseries; the Elmer Myers soon will be. If these two varieties live up to present promises and do not show faults of which we are not yet aware, they will mark another advance in the culture of the black walnut. The truly thin shell

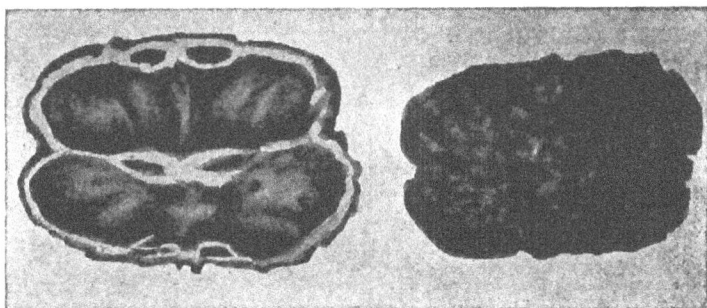

FIGURE 27—THE ELMER MYERS BLACK WALNUT

This variety has the thinnest shell of any black walnut the author has found. When grown in the Pacific Northwest it has cracked exceedingly well, so is one of the most promising of several new blacks. Shell on left has kernel removed.

of the Elmer Myers, which around the cracking edges is not heavier than the shell of a Barcelona filbert, is a surprise to those who have worked with blacks all their lives.

The best cracking nuts by far are the sport type, single lobed nuts sometimes called peanut type nuts. However, none of them seems to have taken the growers' favor. The nuts have but a half nut that usually comes out whole. The Throp, Blættner and Worthington are single lobed, peanut type nuts.

One of the overlooked sections of the country for the black walnut is the Great Salt Lake Basin. Black walnuts are not native there. When the Mormons made the great trek to Utah they carried with them walnuts from Illinois. They must have been selected nuts. A progressive grower there wanted something better so he sent for some Thomas trees. When they bore he found he did not have anything better than some of the native nuts. The Thomas nuts were small and so were all the nuts of black walnut trees that grow there. But an investigation showed that several locals were better than the Thomas.

The grower heard of one that cracked out whole. A hundred mile trip showed no nuts for he found the owner of the tree had cracked them all and stored the meats for family use. But about a third of the nut kernels had come from the nut whole. Now the tree has been taken care of and small trees grafted. It will probably go by the name of Stuart. As the Thomas nuts grew smaller when the variety was moved in the Salt Lake region, the Stuart may be expected to make a much larger nut in a more favorable climate. It might change its character as it comes out of that region, but if better than the Thomas there, it should be better than the Thomas anywhere.

The Deming Purple black walnut, with reddish shades in deep green foliage during the summer, is one of the most beautiful of all trees. It does not give the bizarre effect of the odd color of the blue spruce or the bright colors of the Japanese maple, but fits into the background like the colored shadows that some old Dutch painters put in their landscapes. A heavy bearer of average nuts, with purple pellicle on the kernels, it is one of the finest ornamental trees ever discovered.

Some groves are planted, and more will be, of grafted black walnuts. There is limited market for them in the shell and a strong demand for the meats. The place for the groves will probably be in farm lots where trees can be grown for timber and at the same time furnish nuts for the family and for market. Prices are not high enough to justify great expenditures and the buyers, as most buyers anywhere, buy as cheaply as possible. Where many are selling, the prices drop low. We Americans buy wheat, corn, and rice at ten and twelve or fifteen dollars a bushel when it is cooked in flakes or blown up with hot air. We buy what the advertising man would label as "psychological satisfaction." When growers are trying to sell something as good as a black walnut, which is a rich food, with a cooking flavor many of us prefer to vanilla, they fail to get what they should. They "have something" but they will have to make buyers believe it. Plenty of Americans are yet left to buy if the black walnut kernels were put on the market where they could be bought in small packages for the city home.

THE JAPANESE HEARTNUT

One walnut almost unknown in this country but certain to find favor with the nut trade is the Japanese heartnut, a sport form of the Japanese walnut, which in its original type is a hardshelled poor cracking nut. Occasional seedling trees of the Japanese walnut bear these heart-shaped nuts that break easily along the lines on the outside of the heart. The kernel comes out whole when a heartnut is properly cracked. The nut has a mild flavor that resembles American butternut. The largest nuts are an inch and a quarter long and an inch across.

The trees are wide spreading with long drooping leaf stems that suggest tropical foliage. They are fast growing and bear heavily. Some of the

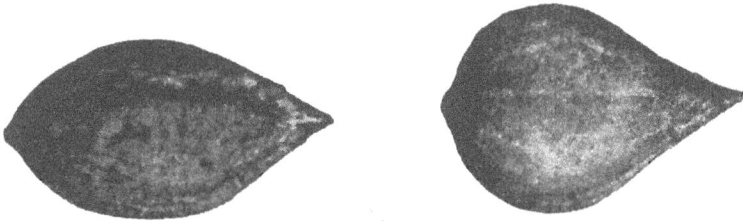

FIGURE 28—JAPANESE WALNUT AND HEARTNUT SPORT

At the left is the ordinary, hard shell, Japanese walnut, difficult to crack and remove the kernels without breaking them up small. The Gellatly No. 2, at the right, is the long type of heartnut, sport of the Japanese walnut.

varieties are hardy and do well in Canada while others seem better adapted to warmer climates, as far south as the Carolinas. So far no disease has been reported attacking this tree.

With the heartnut we have been limited in planting by the number of trees available. This is partly because they do not propagate easily. They have been grafted upon American black walnut root but do not always make a vigorous tree on that root. On the California black root they seem much better but this root would not be safe to plant east of the Cascades. It does not appear that any nurseryman has succeeded in propagating them upon the Japanese root successfully enough to be profitable. This is sure to be worked out in time.

Seedlings of the heartnut do not come true to type. Usually the seedling produces nuts of the ordinary hard cracking Japanese walnut. Sometimes they give butternut type nuts indicating that the bloom was pollinized by a butternut. Some seedlings in our nursery suggest that they are hybrids of the Japanese and the English walnut. Some seem to be crossed with American black walnut. But as we have never brought any of these to bearing we do not know what the resulting nut may be like.

The ability of the Japanese walnut to cross with any of the rest of the walnut family offers a fascinating field for breeders of nut trees. Pollination with the heartnut for crops seems a simple problem though we are sure that some varieties will not pollinize themselves as the male blooms do not always cover the period of the opening of the female nut blooms. They have immense, long catkins with abundant pollen. A few varieties together will furnish pollen during all the blooming period.

There are at least a dozen good varieties of heartnuts in the United States but only a few are

FIGURE 29—HEARTNUT TREE IN BLOOM

Notice the great number of long catkins. This tree is on the experiment farm of the Department of Agriculture at Arlington, Virginia. Photo, courtesy of Department of Agriculture.

propagated by nurserymen. The Fodermaier is a large, plump nut which originated in New York State but it may bloom a little too early for good pollination. Faust is a broad nut, large and smooth and has borne heavily. The Gellatly No.

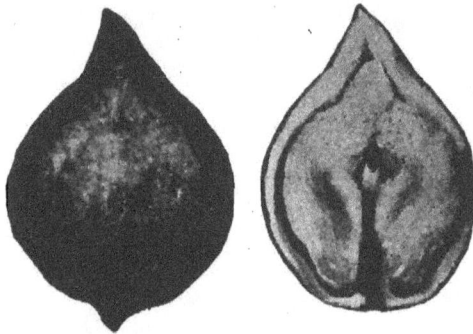

FIGURE 30—FAUST HEARTNUT

By a blow on its side, the Faust heartnut breaks around the outside of the heart, so the kernel may be picked out whole.

2, originated in British Columbia, is a long slim nut. The Wright is a first class nut that originated in western New York.

To those who wish to gamble on a future crop the heartnut offers a promising opportunity. Here we have a nut with real cracking quality, fine flavor, heavy producing varieties, hardy trees, and disease-free, as far as we know. Of course, the trees are slow, there is no immediate market for the nuts, and methods of cleaning and polishing must be worked out. These last present no great problems. The unusual shape of the nut, its easy cracking and superb flavor would attract and hold customers. What a nut it would make for the Valentine Day trade!

THE BUTTERNUT

The butternut is known as the hardiest of the large American nut trees of North America. It is found over the northern states from the Atlantic Coast to the Missouri River. Much like the black walnut in appearance it is more slender and does not make as large a tree nor does it make so fast a growth. The wood is good for cabinet work with a light unusual color and grain but does not have the durability nor rich beauty of the black walnut. Considerable of the colonial furniture was made of butternut. The pioneers also used the bark to make a brown dye. The tree grows on river bottoms and will stand a high water table.

The nut is long, ordinary specimens exceeding two inches, and a little less than half as thick as long. The shell is heavy with a large proportion of shell to kernel. However, the kernels are large and, in the good varieties, often come from the shell in full halves. A few will crack out better than the average black walnut.

As the name suggests the flavor is mild and rich.

It is often the favorite nut of those who grew up where the nut was growing wild. In stores in sections where it grows and in some of the fancy groceries of the cities, there is sale for the butternut. The nut is dried in the tight-sticking husk and sold thus, except in a few instances where it has been run through a machine to remove the husk and smooth the rough, sharp surface.

The place for the butternut is in the farm woodlot, as a dual purpose, ornamental-nut tree and for the reforestation in creek bottoms. The selected varieties are considerably better than average seedlings but are not too good as yet. Grafting the butternut in the eastern United States has proved a problem but on the Pacific Coast it does not seem so stubborn, though we do not always have good stands, where trees are grafted in the nursery.

Of the varieties grown, Thill is a fairly good nut and bears well. Deming from Connecticut has borne early and will probably be a heavy bearer. Aiken seems a heartnut hybrid from its growth, bark, and foliage, though the nut appears to be pure butternut. Buckley from Iowa should be among the hardiest.

We know little about their pollination but most butternut trees grown in groups are heavy bearing trees in the midwest butternut country.